Finding Father

Written by Jack Gabolinscy
Illustrated by Lachlan Creagh

I waited for my father's ship to come home, but it never arrived.

Many ships came, but not the *Sun Queen*. She was a barque, with three masts and large square sails. She left for Australia on January 9, 1852. She should have been home in August. Now it was September. I missed Father so much. I thought about him every day.

I watched and waited and worried. I thought of all the bad things that might happen. Ships can sink in storms, crash onto rocks, and be attacked by pirates.

"When will Father come?" I asked my mother.

Mother stopped feeding Baby Annie. "Don't worry, James. Maybe he'll be home tomorrow," she said. But he wasn't.

September passed and October came. The sun left and the bitter cold arrived. I wore boots and a long coat to keep warm. Every day, I listened for the sound of Father's heavy footfall on the wooden steps outside.

I asked my brother, William, "When will Father come home?"

William looked worried, but he said, "I'm sure Father will be home soon."

I remembered what Father had told me when he left. He had stood in the doorway in his black captain's cap, holding his heavy, wooden sailor's trunk. "You and William must look after Mother and Baby Annie 'til I come home, James," he said.

But what if Father never came home? Could William and I look after our mother and the baby without him?

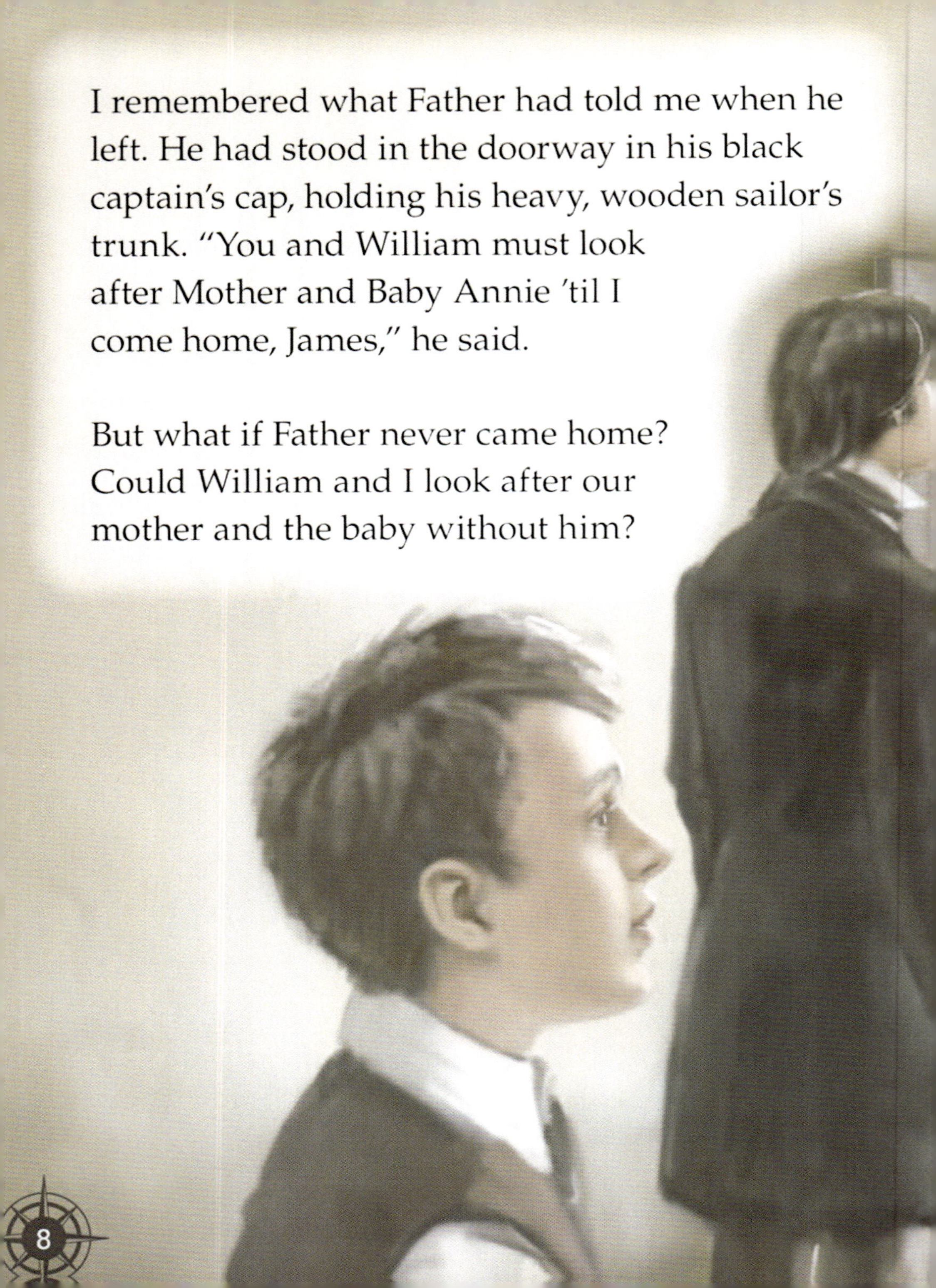

There was a full moon that night. Lying in bed, I could see William moving around in the dark. I heard him stuffing things into a bag. Then, I heard two thumps as he pulled on his boots. Finally, he put on his coat.

"James," William whispered, "I am going to Australia to find Father."

I lit a candle and asked myself, "What would Father do if William or I were lost?" I knew the answer.

"Take me with you, William," I begged.

I took some bread from the kitchen and filled a leather bottle with water from the pump. I took all the pocket money I had left. Finally, I left a note on the kitchen table.

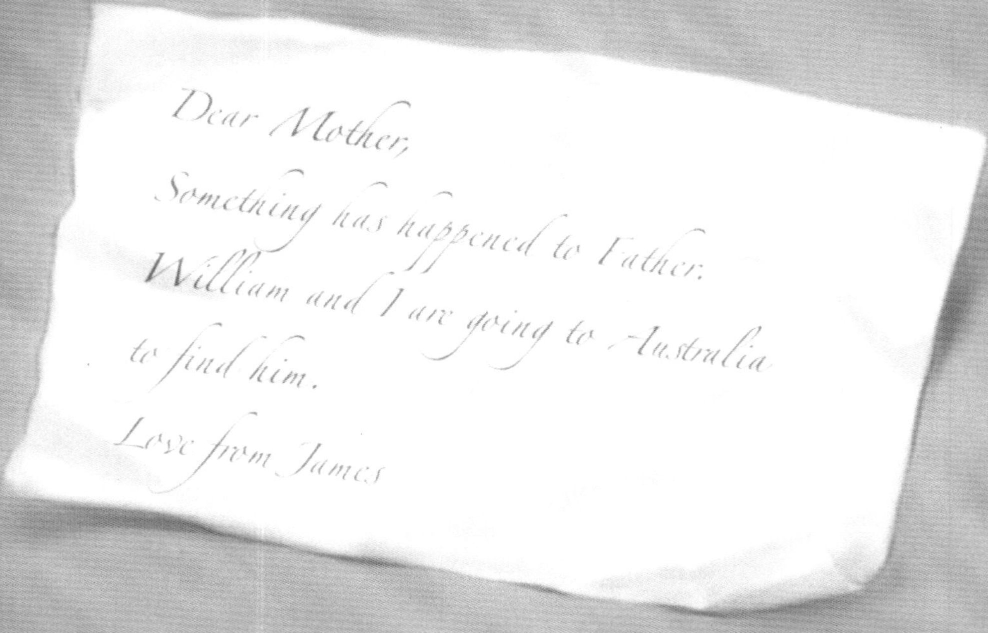

We hurried through the dark streets. A ship named *Sea Friend* was at the wharf. Two men were talking loudly as they loaded supplies onto the ship's deck in the dim light. We heard one of the men say the ship was leaving for Australia.

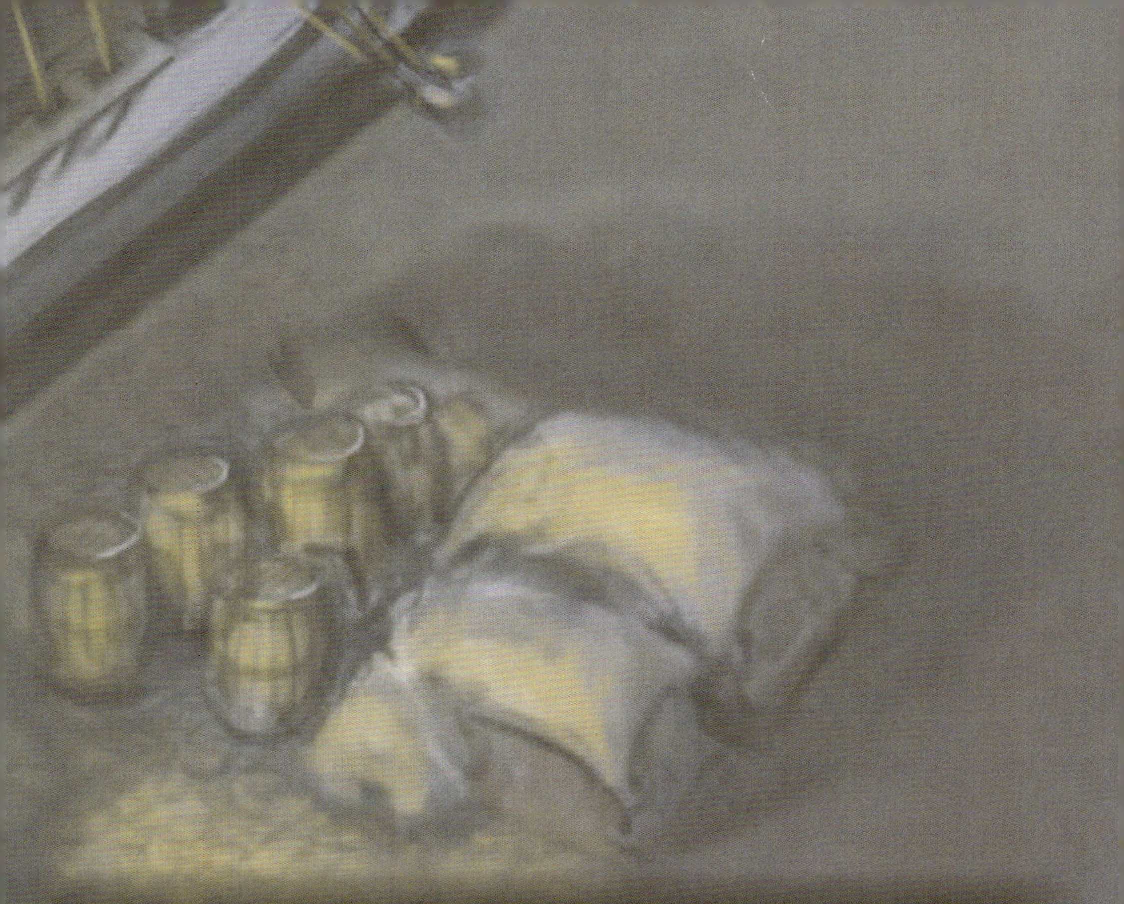

Everyone was too busy to notice us moving through the shadows. We crept up the gangplank, along the deck, down some stairs, and into an empty storeroom. The storeroom was as dark as a coalmine.

Soon, we felt the ship moving. "We're coming, Father," I said. Then, I fell asleep, huddled against William on the storeroom floor.

My brother and I hid in the storeroom for three days. The ship tossed about on the waves like a toy boat. Our hungry tummies rumbled like distant thunder.

On the fourth day, the door suddenly opened. A big man came in. "A-ha!" he said when he saw us. "Stowaways! I'll feed you to the sharks!"

The man took us to the captain. His cabin was big and tidy, with windows looking out onto the sea. He was looking at a map covered with lines and numbers and pictures of far-off lands.

"What's your name, boy?" the captain growled at me.

"James Tar, sir," I said. "This is my brother, William. Our father is captain of the *Sun Queen*. She didn't come home from Australia. We're going to find him."

The captain stopped looking angry. "You tried to go all the way to Australia to rescue your father? You boys are too young for a big adventure like that. Do you even know where your father is? Australia's a big place. What were you planning to do?"

Then, the captain smiled. "You're a brave couple of boys. I know why the *Sun Queen* didn't come home. She hit a rock and nearly sank. She's in Sydney being fixed. The crew was rescued just in time."

The captain grinned at the big man. "Sorry, cook. You can't feed the Tar brothers to the sharks. They can work for you in the kitchen 'til we reach Australia."

The cook nodded, then smiled down at me. "I didn't really plan to feed you to the sharks, you know," he said.

The cook and I became good friends. I worked hard in the kitchen. I peeled potatoes, cleaned pots and pans, and wiped down tables for the hungry sailors.

But sometimes, there was no work to do. Then, I would clamber over to the bow of the ship, stand with the sun and wind on my face, and think of Australia.

Today, I was thinking about Mother, Father, and Baby Annie. I hoped it wouldn't be too long before we were all together again. I stood in the warm sun, faced into the wind, and smiled.